FRANCIS

Ann Wroe

FRANCIS: A LIFE IN SONGS

JONATHAN CAPE
LONDON

3 5 7 9 10 8 6 4 2

Jonathan Cape, an imprint of Vintage Publishing,
20 Vauxhall Bridge Road,
London SW1V 2SA

Jonathan Cape is part of the Penguin Random House group of companies
whose addresses can be found at global.penguinrandomhouse.com.

Penguin
Random House
UK

First published by Jonathan Cape in 2018

penguin.co.uk/vintage

A CIP catalogue record for this book is available from the British Library

ISBN 9781787331488

Typeset in 11/15 pt Dante MT
by Integra Software Services Pvt. Ltd, Pondicherry

Printed and bound by L.E.G.O S.p.A, Vicenza, Italy

Cover: Saint Francis from a fresco, Sacro Speco, Subiaco © Photo Scala,
Florence, courtesy of the Ministero Beni e Att. Culturali e del Turismo

Penguin Random House is committed to a sustainable future
for our business, our readers and our planet. This book is made
from Forest Stewardship Council® certified paper.

For Mark

FOREWORD

There have been many lives of St Francis. My only excuse for this one is that it is written in songs; because it struck me, when I began to consider writing his biography, that his was a life lived in poetry rather than prose.

Each subject-heading falls into four parts. First come quotations from the earliest sources, and from Francis himself, to provide a narrative thread and to fix the mental context of the time. Two poems follow: the first an evocation of Francis at this point or in this aspect, the second a reflection of this aspect of him in the modern world. A short grace-note, a Franciscan echo in Nature that could be then, or could be now, links each subject to the next.

The metre of the poems that evoke Francis himself is deliberately four-beat on almost all occasions. This was a common rhythm for the troubadour songs he loved; and it is also a conscious evocation of the fourfold sign of the Cross which, after his conversion, was the immovable centre and structure of his life.

CONTENTS

SCENE FROM CHILDHOOD

He was stamped with Christ's brilliant seal.

Thomas di Celano, *Life of St Francis 2*, ix

Beneath this wall of sainted stones
you stop, look up. You know just where
a tremor starts along your bones—
where ghostly fingers lift your hair.

An angel stands at Heaven's gates,
his robes stiff-pleated like a fan
by far-off winds. And as he waits,
with one straight hand he brands a man.

Ferociously he stares at you—
but sometimes, in a different sun,
as lovingly as mothers do
when their commands are left undone

but they forgive you. With his wings
close folded round, a feathered shawl,
his thumb digs in. Meanwhile, he sings.
His victim makes no cry at all.

CONVERSION

CONVERSION

THE CALL

*[As the son of Pietro Bernadone, a rich cloth-merchant of Assisi],
Francis was the ringleader of Assisi's frivolous young crowd. He
once gave a sumptuous dinner ... and while the others dirtied
the streets with their drunken songs, he followed them, carrying
a staff in his hand. But gradually he withdrew bodily as he had
already turned deaf mentally to those things, while he sang to
the Lord in his heart.*

*So much divine sweetness poured over him ... that he was
struck dumb and could not move. A burst of spiritual energy
rushed through him, snatching him into the unseen ...*

Celano, *Remembrance of the Desire of a Soul* 1, iii

*'If I had been pricked all over, as if with knives, I couldn't have
moved from the spot.'*

Francis in *The Legend of St Francis*
by the Three Companions, 7

The message came in bales of cloth.
You packed those up in sacking bags,
trussed them with rope,
sent them away.
You'd open them another day.

The message came in clash of arms,
that moment when your heart flew up
with your home flag.
You fought it off.
War-cries were ordinance enough.

The message came in dregs of wine
knocked over on a linen cloth,
crimson on white.
You broke your song
an instant, then you carried on.

But now in drunk stone-stumbling dark
it grabs your feet, and drives your staff
deep in sweet ground.
And so, staved through,
you ask Him what to do.

São Martinho, Portugal

The day it happened, friends at a café table
waited with glasses filled as I came in
dazzled with light, but not from the road or the sand,
dry as a traveller from the desert, but not for the drink
they laughingly pushed towards me; parched, desperate,
    famished,
but not for that—
only for ink, wine-sour and black enough
to mark my pulses down before they vanished,
only for paper, pure, white, cool,
sheet upon crisp sheet, empty, or any scrap
pulled from a saving pocket like bread, or life.

The call
without words
is one
the feet obey
even
before
the heart

LEPERS

Francis was converted around 1207, when he was twenty-five.

While still in the clothes of the world, he met a leper one day. Made stronger than himself, he dismounted from his horse ... and ran to kiss him.

Celano, *Life* 1, vi; *Remembrance of the Desire of a Soul* 1, v

'When I was in sin, it seemed too bitter to me to see lepers, and the Lord himself led me among them ... And when I left them, what had seemed bitter was changed for me into sweetness of body and soul. And afterwards I remained a little and I left the world.'

Francis, *Testament*

Your horse left on the grassy verge
crops unconcerned,
reins loose. In an adjoining field
earth's overturned;
a ploughman whistles careless songs,
his hat tipped low.
And you, what are you doing here?
You hardly know
where in this scene you should belong,
distant or near,
staying or fleeing; fending off
contagious fear
with both imploring hands, or else
embracing it;
fainting at leper-stink, or else
hard-chasing it—
But now you kiss that rotting flesh
slow, stomach churned.
Now you press close His bandaged love
stunned, silent, burned.

In an adjoining field
earth's overturned.

He's given wide berth in the checkout queue
at Morrison's; the stench of ancient piss
makes the girl sniff. Lank threads of greying hair
straggle from underneath a Russian hat;
his jeans fray to the floor, and every ripped
vent in his coat shows lining poking through,
curiously clean. Puddings are all he's bought:
jam mini-sponges, Danish cherry slice,
fruit-corner yogurts, finding sweetness there
he won't get otherwise. Job done, he goes
shakily, stiffly out, pausing with care
to count his change into a banker's bag.
Within the beard, his delicate small lips
murmur a silent word—might take a kiss—

Thrown out,
the flour-sack
scarecrow
spreads ever-open arms;
wears
resurrection
white

AT SAN DAMIANO

With his heart already completely changed ... he was walking one day by the church of San Damiano near Assisi, which was abandoned by everyone and almost in ruins. Led by the Spirit, he went in to pray and knelt down devoutly before the crucifix. Then ... with the lips of the painting, the image of Christ crucified spoke to him. 'Francis,' it said, calling him by name, 'go and rebuild my house; as you see, it is all being destroyed.' Francis was like a man out of his senses ... but pulled himself together to obey ...

From that time on, compassion for the Crucified was impressed into his holy soul, and the wounds of the Passion were stamped deep in his heart. He could not hold back his tears ... but went through Assisi begging for oil to fill the lamps in San Damiano.

Celano, *Remembrance of the Desire of a Soul* 1, vi, viii

'In pictures of God and the Blessed Virgin painted on wood, God and the Blessed Virgin are honoured ... yet the wood and paint ascribe nothing to themselves, because they are just wood and paint. ... So the servant of God is a kind of painting ... that is, a creature of God who can ascribe nothing to himself.'

Francis in *Scripta Leonis*, 104

'Most High and Glorious God, enlighten the dark places of my heart.'

Prayer of Francis before the crucifix of San Damiano

You come to kneel in penitence.
Here is the tree. Here is your Lord
nailed up like some corn-stealing bird,
eyes dulled, wings splayed. Thin streams of blood
run scarlet from His feet and hands.
You're crying now. You're crying now.

It is an image done on wood.
That's all. Yet through your falling tears
He trembles into light, Who sent
these tears to you. Half-conscious sighs
that leave your lips now breathe from His,
incense and words, His name and yours,

and you who were mere paint and wood,
a senseless thing, begin to feel
love-notes that stir within your spine
and shiver upwards, tuning you
to bliss or agony like His
against the grain, against the grain,

then as new buds swell through the bark
like oil in spring, chill sweat breaks out
on His brow, yours, till your dead wood
turns soft as His, and you leap up
full-leafed towards that blazing grace—
The nails are sharp in His embrace.

San Damiano, April

At last at San Damiano the storm broke,
flushing the roads to rivers. On our right

a handmade sign stood propped beside a stall,
Vendesi olio nuovo: not a sight

expected at this season of the year,
or in such weather. Maybe it was old;

it had that look; or maybe it referred
to pressings never-ending, to the cold-

crushing of new-crop sainthood, over there
in that dark vault sunk in an olive grove,

obscured by windscreen-wipers in the rain:
from bruising wood, gold welling drops of love.

Before this tree
split
lightning-deep,
a stream
keeps silence,
and the birds
also

SMALL CHURCHES

The first work he undertook was to build a house of God. He did not try to build a new one, but repaired an old one ... The Church of the Blessed Virgin at Portiuncula ['the little portion'] was deserted, and no one was taking care of it ... He began to stay there continually, and the restoration of the church took place in the third year of his conversion.

Celano, *Life* 1, iv, ix

Of old it was called St Mary of the Angels because, it was said, the songs of angels and celestial spirits were heard by those who came there.

Mirror of Perfection, lv

When he went through the villages in the neighbourhood of Assisi ... he carried a broom to sweep the churches. For he was very sad when he entered any church and found it was not clean.

Scripta Leonis, 18

'Brothers should always build small churches; and the tiny churches will preach to them, and they will be more edified by these than by words.'

Francis in *Mirror of Perfection*, x

La Portiuncula, Sta Maria dei Angeli, Assisi

Moored rocking
                in these angels' woods
the upside-down
                stone hammered hull
of your small ship,
                smoothed inside, out,
with sweat, with love,
                by reverent hands
of those who board
                to sail with you:
to curl in that
                inverted place
ballast of prayer
                hauled overhead,
new-Brother hearts
                surrendering
to holy, holy,
                holy waves;
your guiding lamp
                within, without,
fast-anchored
                in a vault of stars.

Good Shepherd, Lullington, East Sussex

Last stones of the abandoned nave
graze quiet as sheep in half-mown grass,
moss on their backs. A leaning grave
speaks low of lichened holiness.

No path is worn towards the door.
Bright stitchwork on the western wall
blesses the sixteen chairs. A score
of hymn books wait. A priest will call

three times a year, and on those days
the cramped harmonium's played, the damp-
paged Bible shaken out, mauve sprays
of mallow picked, and in the lamp

new candles jammed. Folk never seen
file up the path from Alfriston
or park upon the upper green,
until with screeching wheels they're gone—

and dust returns. Last minims spent
infuse the fabric of the place.
Lost spectacles left on the font
continue to enquire for grace.

The brisk new broom
brushes light in
as dead leaves out:
alert light, awaiting
some eye,
some footfall,
like bright flowers
left
on a window sill

POPPIES

In his youth he had endeavoured to surpass others in his flamboyant display of vain accomplishments: wit, curiosity, practical jokes and foolish talk, songs, and soft flowing garments ... He enjoyed wearing scarlet robes.

Celano, *Life* 1, i, vii

Now, as Brothers joined him, he ordered them to shun fine fabrics [especially scarlet cloth], and those who acted to the contrary he rebuked publicly with biting words.

Celano, *Life* 2, xxxix

That blood-red cloth you loved to wear
flowers now among the summer fields.
Pick out a sample if you dare,
rough-crush it in your fist; it yields
                    (so easily creasing
                    with grasp and releasing!)
then half-springs back, fine crimson stuff
loose-crumpled with a dirty stain.
Harsh handling cures you soon enough;
but touch, and you may fall again.
                    (So preening in scarlet,
                    robes of the harlot!)
Their beauty draws the pale-winged fly,
moths hovering at dusk, the bee
that tumbles past, cold raindrops' sly
quick salutations, and the free
                    (so delicate, taunting,
                    turning and flaunting!)
flirtation of the dancing wind—
and you, who, trudging dustily
your praying path, still sigh to find
these wantons in your company.

The day was foggy, I remember it;
thick, clammy on the tops. But lower down

it cleared to drizzling fields, crabbed alder trees,
an old man strimming in the sunken lane.

And as we cleared the stile beside the house
unheralded a thousand poppies blazed

across the sweeping lawns, for no clear cause
that we discerned—for passers-by who gazed

impertinent, like us, above the wall—
or for the brash corruption of the three

white marble youths, soul-naked, as they stood
oblivious in their godliness, too good,
thigh-deep and deeper in that scarlet sea.

Wind-ravaged
Magdalen,
red flounces gone,
clasps tight
her jade-green
box
of balm

TAKEN FOR A FOOL

When those who knew him saw him, they shouted that he was insane and out of his mind, and threw mud and stones from the streets at him ... but God's servant was deaf to all of them ...

Once, when he was attacked by thieves, he cried confidently: 'I am the herald of the Great King! What is it to you?' They beat him and threw him into a ditch full of deep snow, shouting, 'Lie there, you stupid herald of God!' And he rolled around exhilarated with joy.

Celano, *Life* 1, v, vii

Whenever he wished to do penance he would sit among ashes and rub them in his hair ... He would also sprinkle them on his food, saying to the Brothers: 'Brother Ash is pure.'

Three Companions, 15, *passim*

To wear repentance like a robe
or like a cloak
obscuring every part of you,
you would unhook
the mourning clouds from winter skies
and pull them on,
strap round dry strips of sickled fields,
their harvest gone,
or writhe contrition like the sea,
one wave of pain.
Your grief's the world's, your folly too.
They are the same.
But since your sorrow's hemmed about
by frailty,
you crouch instead beside the hearth,
half-crazily
scooping and smearing debris round
your face and hair,
your legs, your arms, until you are
ash everywhere:
tear-drenched within your coat of woe,
absolving snow.

As strange ones go they classed him at the margin,
some sort of random clown,
riding the sideways seats, dressed lawyerly,
at least from collar down,

but with his face daubed plaster-white, as if
to play a tragic role,
and wide sad eyes smudged round with black mascara—
a tart, or a lost soul.

A violin case was all his worldly luggage,
stuffed full of tricks no doubt:
a gun, as in that film, or flock of pigeons,
if he dared let them out,

white rabbits, sprays of fireworks, billowing scarves
tossed upwards endlessly—
or a strobe light, on everyone's dark corners
to glare alarmingly.

So passengers as one turned to the windows,
turned from that staring mask;
did not approach, or beg him to do magic.
Much too dangerous to ask.

Grabbed earthwards
by a sparrow,
the butterfly
has only
his
provocative
oddity
to blame

FOX-SKIN

He made himself a tunic ... which was very rough, so that by wearing it he might crucify the flesh with its vices and sins. He made it very poor and plain, a thing the world would never covet.

Celano, *Life* 1, ix

He once had it patched with fox-skin both inside and out, for he said: 'If you want me to put up with this under my tunic, have another piece of the same size sewn on the outside, telling people that a piece of fur is hidden underneath.'

Celano, *Remembrance of the Desire of a Soul* 1, xciii

The particular brown of his habit was called, by the Umbrian peasants, 'beast colour'.

This tunic laid out under glass—
the one they say is yours—dried flat,
patched up, like some old fox's pelt
crushed on the road, wind-worried-over,
carrion for crows; or sacking left
smelling of rot and fizzing pulp,
when windfall apples have been chopped
and mangled through it—this same robe,
once doors are locked and candles blown,
gathers itself in threadbare joy,
shakes out its sleeves and whirls around,
a Christ-dance over holy ground.

We noticed the crows first.
Shouting, with blue-black wings hunched round their heads,
accusing beaks. Fluttering, not flying
from tilted gatepost and redundant wire,
as if snagged there. Then following the line
of eye and wing we saw, stock-still,
the fox. Dark, immature and lean,
uncertain in his rough brown skin,
beast-colour. Briefly he paused
in the wide tableau of the stubble field,
victim-in-waiting—till he found
purpose and pace, loped, ran,
and running turned invisible, sliding
into the earth-tones, under the hedge, no trace;
triumphant in some harsh and pricking place.

Despised
in
the sinews
of the city,
the beggar-fox
trails
his trembling wildness
like a smell
from house to house

MONEY

Francis taught the Brothers to tread money underfoot like dust, and to weigh it at the same price and weight as asses' dung.

Three Companions, 45

He used to call coins 'flies'.

Celano, *Remembrance of the Desire of a Soul* 2, xxxv, xlvii

'You ought to go for alms more willingly and joyfully than he who for one piece of money returns a hundred pence, since you are offering people the love of God.'

Francis in *Mirror of Perfection,* 18

The money in that purse is theirs.
It's light as sheep-shit, pattering down
from flocks on roads. You'd rather roll
goat pellets round your mouth, lick off
dry pigeon lime dripped down a wall,
suck up slime-trails of chicken dung
splattering a yard, than touch it. Leave
their scat for them to revel in:
to count up carefully, hands filled
and filthier with each one, as from
some cesspit rim—

           Offer them this.
God's love held out in empty palms,
uncountable, uncounted alms.

Office windowsill, London

Unwanted pennies, week by week pulled out
from pockets, make up this memorial hoard
stowed in a plastic cup. No one's about
to empty it, or count them; they are stored
purely for lightness' sake, the pleasing glow
of shedding them. Yet they're not thrown away,
and by their long accumulation grow
heavy again, though no one here can say
what they are worth, or whether they have worth
if no one spends them.
                            Just so, on a day
mizzling with rain, tangy with fresh-turned earth,
a man crept past me with a plastic cup,
the twin to this, filled with his father's ash—
fearing to throw it, summoning up
courage to see it valueless, a dash
of dark on the unknowing wind,
less than the coins we leave behind.

Begged
for
hard cash,
the wise
hand over
softer
tender

BREAD

'Bread is truly angels' food, when it is begged for the love of God.'
Francis in Bonaventure, *Life*, vii, 8

Towards the sacrament of the Lord's Body he burned with fervour to his very marrow, and with unbounded wonder at that loving condescension, and condescending love.

Celano, *Life* 2, clii

'We have nothing and we see nothing of the Most High in this world except His Body and Blood.'

Francis, *First Rule*

He condescends as bread:
your Lord whose power
could shrivel up the land
now lingers light
within a poor priest's hand.

He condescends like this:
your Lord whose dread
storm-servants scour the street,
is mutely laid
in mouths foul-furred with sleep.

He condescends as bread:
your Lord who flung
flame-stars like stones around,
accepts the tongue
with which He's pressed and ground.

He condescends like this:
your Lord who bends
Fate to His whirling will,
for His dear ends
enters you, and is still.

From the back-sanctuary of flour and steam
two men in white caps carry new-batch loaves
swaddled in cloths, each one still breathing-warm:

char-crusted sourdough honeycombed with air,
gilded baguettes crisp-splitting to the knife,
nibbed hazelnut as dense as fossil-stone,

silk-crumb brioche. We hunker down on these
at planking tables, peasants bulking out
our Guatemalan, mocha, filter, foam....

He moves among us, hunger in his look.
The home-made leaflets in his veiny hand
are poems. They cost nothing. Four of them

on one pink folded sheet. They're quickly read.
They may sustain us longer than this bread.

All day the sun has baked
the hillsides, and the raked
wheatfields which curve and lie
under a cope of sky;
the eagle, dipping slow,
breathes incense from below.

OBEDIENCE

[1209]

When Francis saw that God was daily increasing his followers, he wrote for himself and his Brothers ... a Form of Life and a Rule.... He then went to Rome, as he greatly desired that the Lord Pope Innocent III should confirm for him what he had written.... And the pope gave his assent to his request, exhorting and then warning them about many things ...

Celano, *Life* 1, xiii

When the Pope first looked at Brother Francis, with his mean appearance ... he was filled with contempt, and said: 'Go, Brother, look for some pigs ... and roll yourself in the muck with them.' When Francis heard this he bowed his head, went straight out, found some pigs ...

Matthew Paris, *Chronica Majora*
(in John R.H. Moorman (ed.), *New Fioretti*, p. 43)

'A dead body does not complain about where it is put, does not resist being moved ... This is someone who really obeys.'
Francis in Celano, *Remembrance of the Desire of a Soul* 2, cxii

Obedience
has crossed keys on his shoes.
His throne is marble. You must kiss
the hand extended, and the ring
big as a walnut. Kiss the ring.

> *Holy Obedience sent you here*
> *unwashed, unshaven, as you are.*

Obedience
presides in libraries of bulls.
Each one is labelled. Each declares
You Must Not, or perhaps You May.
Bowed minions feather dust away.

> *Holy Obedience binds your cord*
> *neck, breast and ankles to the Lord.*

Obedience's thrice-crowned head
thrice nods assent. His cardinals
already turn disdainful backs.
Strange little man, you've said your piece;
through this great door lies your release.

> *Holy Obedience makes you run*
> *to join the beggars in the sun.*

High Line, New York City

They sit in scattered quiet
out in the open, under sapling trees
or in the ornamental grass,
legs tucked or crossed, each child
set with a sketchbook. What they draw
is more or less the same: glass towers,
East River, foreground plants in pots,
a boat. All as their teacher sees it, and they know
his world-view should be theirs. Yet one
has lost her heart to mauve and green, and these
hold sway across her page, all forms
blocked fiercely out in them, beneath
a rampant green-mauve sky.
She smiles at me as I walk by.

Subservient
to wind and tide
the cutter
tacks,
more closely to inhabit
each high storm-surge
of the sea

AT RIVO TORTO

In a dream he [had been] led to a very fine palace, full of knightly armour, glittering shields and other apparel, and was told ... that the palace and everything in it belonged to him and his knights.

Three Companions, 5

He gathered with them in a place called Rivo Torto, near the city of Assisi. In this place there was an abandoned hut. Under its shelter lived these despisers of great and beautiful houses, protecting themselves from the torrents of rain ... and lacking everything.

Celano, *Life* 1, xvi

'When the Lord gave me some Brothers, no one showed me what to do.'

Francis, *Testament*

This hut does not belong to you.
That's good. The tumbled struts were once
a livestock place. Sour grassy-warm
their breath in here, the trampled floor
pungent and deep. The little group
you've driven in, King Arthur's knights,
Bernard and Philip, Giles, the rest,
huddle as cattle do, heads down,
hoods past their eyes. No longer is
their world the counting house, the courts,
commerce, esteem, a wife. It's this.
Their names are on the beams, the beams
the Cross. Outside, it rains.

Abandoned shack, Romney Marsh, Kent

The aged shepherd had in his possession
this rust-red shed of corrugated iron;
eight wethers with the grey sky in their fleeces;
brambles, a ditch, a chimney-stack of stone.

One wicker-chair worn ragged with his sitting;
a hoard of pilchards and of HP beans;
one black umbrella for field visitations,
a dozen illustrated magazines.

And in a wooden box beside the fireplace
a trove of nothing in five empty jars;
but in the sixth, a tin for liver tablets;
and in the tin a fragment of the stars.

MISSION

THE GREETING

He went round the towns and villages, sowing the seed of divine blessings everywhere.

Celano, Life 1, xxii

He always said 'Il Signore vi dia pace,' 'May the Lord give you peace,' to all those he met and to those who met him. This formula ... was revealed to him by the Lord ... Since people had never before heard such a greeting given by a religious, they were surprised and some were almost indignant, but he said, 'Let them talk.'

Mirror of Perfection, xxvi; Scripta Leonis, 67

Through evening streets
becalmed by bells
a knight rides in.

His retinue,
cords round their waists,
trail after him.

From haunted hills
he ventures here,
and burning sky

holds like a tree
his hollowed shape
as he goes by.

None welcomes him,
but one nailed door
concedes a crack;

as he cries 'Peace!'
night-feathered fears
shrink silent back.

Firle Beacon, East Sussex, December

Close-passing on the high defile
we offer 'Hallos' and a smile

short-circuited by breath and frost;
dispersed as soon as said, like lost

wing-flickering cries of swift or swallow—

But now we're haloed in live sun,
sharp-focused as the nail-etched thorn

for one bright beat, though our thoughts head
down different paths past grave-mound dead

smooth-hallowing us, as we too hallow.

First rays:
the birch woods'
uncombed hair
stirs,
turns
towards
arriving light

VIOLS IN THE WOODS

'Who are the servants of the Lord, unless they are in some way his minstrels?'

Francis in *Scripta Leonis*, 43

Sometimes ... a sweet melody of the spirit bubbling up inside him would become a French tune on the outside; the thread of a divine whisper which his ears heard secretly would break out in a French song of joy ...

At other times—as I saw with my own eyes—he would pick up a stick from the ground and put it over his left arm, while holding a bow bent with a string in his right hand, drawing it over the stick as if it were a viol, performing all the right movements, and in French would sing about the Lord. All this dancing often ended in tears ...

Celano, *Remembrance of the Desire of a Soul 2, xc*

[One day] there appeared to him an angel who had a viol in his left hand and in his right hand a bow.... The angel drew the bow once across the viol, and immediately ... his soul was inebriated with such sweetness that he thought if the angel had drawn the bow a second time across the strings, his soul would have parted from his body.

Little Flowers of St Francis (Fioretti),
Second Consideration of the Stigmata

Now spring's own woods go robed in green
and chiming birds unloose their throats
to fill each tree with April rain,
the branches staves, the leaves the notes,

as Spirit-words spin out of you,
del temps novel, temps del amor,
a Dieus tot glorios a cantar,
delight you need this language for,

you half-dance past, sticks in your hand
held crosswise, cleaned of bark and pith,
your wonder-viol and aching wand,
mad playthings to make music with;

but if a proper bowl and bow
were sent divinely to you now,
one note, one word would move you so
that you would die, not knowing how.

Tonight faint fumbling chords from a guitar
rise out of someone's garden, in between
the automated clanking of the trains;

the sound of summer, as the thick leaves are,
the shrieks of children up late, and unseen
radios and rows through open windowpanes—

And somehow those insistent echoing strings
weave all the dusk together, creeping thread
connecting star to sky and sky to tree,

shadows to bandstand, diving kite to wings,
stray dog to hill-line, new moon overhead
to loitering lovers in the grassy sea,

their wide unnoticed world bound up entire
by music. And why not our bodies too,
in their least vein and nerve and gleaming hair,

held and sustained by that same silken wire
till the unravelling, when Love draws through
cool breath instead, and the releasing air?

As the reed
for a breath,
so
the string
for a touch
tenses,
waits

THE ROCK-BED

[When he was still in the world] his friends would ask him, 'Do you want to get married, Francis?' He replied: 'I will take a bride more noble and more beautiful than you have ever seen.'

Celano, *Life* 1, iii

He gave up everything that he might cling to Lady Poverty more closely, and the two might be one in spirit. He held her close in chaste embraces, and could not bear to cease being her husband, even for an hour.

Celano, *Remembrance of the Desire of a Soul* 1, xxv

Now as to his bed: the naked ground received his naked body, with only a thin tunic between them ... In the clefts of the rock he would build his nest, and in the hollow of the wall his dwelling.

Celano, *Life* 1, xix, xxvii

Nothing between you now
lying alone.
Nothing at all between
your flesh, her stone.
Her unpinned bracken hair
flung softly brown,
tender-tip curls you kissed
as you sank down,
savouring that hollow
by her smooth breast
whose sweat is yours or hers,
both being undressed;
and this dark chamber-cleft,
narrowest place,
holds you her bondsman bound,
face pressed to face:
love without cease,
without release.

Under a bank, Firle Beacon

To live like a hare
boundless-eyed, leaping

the long brow of the chalk hill—
or lie low, leveret-like

in lush wet cradling
grass beneath the thorn,

sheltered and shaken
under horizontal rain

by these spine-quivering drops
holding all there is

One grey stone
hidden
among multitudes
carries
the sleep-print
of a sea-worm
or
a flower

SERVANT-CREATURES

Even for worms he had a warm love, since he had read this text
about the Saviour: 'I am a worm and not a man.' That is why
he picked up little worms from the road and put them in a safe
place, so they would not be trampled underfoot ... Following the
signs imprinted on creatures, he followed his Beloved everywhere.

Celano, *Remembrance of the Desire of a Soul* 2, cxxiv

'All creatures say and proclaim, God made me for you, O man!'

Francis in *Scripta Leonis,* 51

So delicate
this double
dance,
your fingers round
blind
wriggling
Christ
to rescue Him,
to raise Him safe
as He
from death
has lifted
you

Helpless as a worm, undefended,
the pencil on the track

already bruised and broken-leaded
must be brought safely back—

but in my hand, solicitously cradled,
tilts as a light-forged sword

fine-balanced, poised in power, to channel
flame, or the word.

A violet's
flare
in winter grass
alerts the heart
to other service
unregarded,
almost
missed

SCISSORS

Clare, then eighteen, petitioned to join the Order in 1212. Francis professed her, then installed her at San Damiano to live an enclosed life.

[At San Damiano] Clare threw away all the pleasures and lusts of the world, and gave to the world the word of refusal, and bent her head to the Brothers for the cutting of her hair, and left all her elegances.

> Life and Legend of the Lady St Clare, vi
> (from a French translation by Brother Francis
> du Puis of a lost Latin text, 1563)

You'll cut her hair.
She kneels and turns
to all of you
her small slim back;
you first, with shears
iron-forged to slide
through knotted ties
of any bale,
each shining swatch—

Your left hand clamps
to shoulder-bone
the auburn living
flow, the fall;
your right
parts tresses
from her neck,
thrusts up and through.
                    You will forget
the softness there,
the dimpled nape,
her perfume-sour
and girlish smell.
All's slashed away
for holiness;
all's cut away
as chestnut smoke
swirls, tangles, swathes
the stone-flagged floor.

Right, left. Under, over.
Pull straight. Repeat.
Two plaits.

The child is pale.
The mother stands
well out of eye-range,
above somewhere;
lips pursed
as elastic bands,
red nails
when they intrude
sharp as a slide.

Right, left. Under, over.
Pull straight. Repeat.

Breakfast things
mute on the table,
bowl, spoon, milk carton,
complicit sun
slab-cold. Slat chair
pulled squeaking out.
Late, says the clock,
snap the tugging hands.
Later.

→

Incramming thoughts
of school hard-shined
as unworn leather satchel, shoes.
Closed as these walls.
Unjumpable.

The scraped plaits swing,
pink ribbons on them.
This should be love.
Perhaps it is.

Sunlight
slow-blading
over
tonsures
the hill's
sacred head;
lambs
shiver,
new-shorn

SHEEP

He loved lambs for their guilelessness and simplicity. When he was given one, he exhorted it to praise God straight away …

Bonaventure, *Life*, viii, 7

He would greet sheep graciously, and they would run to him and gaze on him with delight, returning his greeting with loud bleating … He longed also to be a good shepherd, and to lose none of the flock.

Celano, *Treatise on the Miracles*, iv

[He called his favourite, Brother Leo, 'Pecorello di Dio', 'Little Lamb of God', and drew a cartoon blessing for him in which his holy Tau descended on Leo's head …]

This symbol of the Tau he revered with deep affection … and, in the letters that he dictated, signed it with his own hand at the end, as though all his care was, in the prophet's words, to set a mark upon the foreheads of the men who sigh and cry.

Bonaventure, *Life*, iv, 9

Leaning, as any shepherd does,
fatherly over the loud flock
as it swarms in, you touch and bless
each jostling head that pauses, bows
and passes you. You can discern
by scars or skullcaps each man there
as surely as by name or voice;
know him by shaven scalp and hair.

Thus you know Bernard, straight and grey
as beeches are; Elias, grand
as his sleek dome; Big Bruiser John
collared like iron beneath your hand;
Pacifico, so full of songs
that his loose locks vibrate and shine;
and Secretary Leo, keen
to nudge his plumpness up the line.

You drew him as a shepherd would,
stippling that round pincushion head,
scratching affection there, as with
your inky Tau you marked for God
your little lambkin. Reverently
he took and kissed your careful art:
Dominus benedicat, pressed
in four upon his following heart.

Wolstonbury Hill, East Sussex

With scattered chimes as from a sacring bell
young tegs crop grass on Wolstonbury Hill:
acolytes all, heads bent among the coarse
dwarf-thistle, or in candle-flickering gorse,
kneeling to eat. Chill clouds pass overhead,
carrying December in their snow-blue tread;
shadowing tumuli, which one by one
lift up the pallid wafer of the sun;
shadowing beasts, who bow as humans do,
Sanctus at throat and breast, if any knew.

The flock
long gone,
their bleating words
are wisped
in wind
on every hedge

LETTER-GATHERING

He used to gather up any piece of writing, whether divine or human, wherever he found it; on the road, in the house, on the floor. He would reverently pick it up and put it in a sacred or decent place because the name of the Lord, or something pertaining to it, might be written there ...

Celano, *Life* 1, xxix

He dreamed ... that he was gathering tiny breadcrumbs from the ground, which he had to distribute to a crowd of hungry Brothers who stood before him. He was afraid ... that such minute particles would slip through his fingers ... But a voice cried out to him, 'Francis, the crumbs you saw last night are the words of the Gospel ... '

Celano, *Remembrance of the Desire of a Soul* 2, clix

'Those brothers who are ignorant of letters must not labour to learn them, but only to possess the Spirit of the Lord.'

Francis, *Second Rule*

Sometimes the face of Christ
appears in wheat;
each polished grain incised
exact, complete
with His dear mouth and eyes
that you may kiss and greet.

He does not live in books;
He is not found
in parchment, vellum, stacks
of pages bound,
nor bulls with seals attached
and strings tied round.

He lives in every phrase
spilled out like seeds
from muttering-past *Aves*
and fingered beads;
from what a Brother prays,
not what he reads.

And yet torn paper scraps
tossed on the floor
may bear the Word, perhaps,
you hunger for;
harvest of tiny gems,
seed-pearls of holy names,
glean close, close store.

Wide-ruled white paper
covers his small lap
with mysterious marks:
characters that caper,
curl, cling on, trap
long tails, fizz sparks
of not-yet-grasped
importance; and he shouts
their names, loud free
mantras of lessons past,
heedless of whereabouts—
sings in the key
of A, E, F and C,
and R, and T.

A word resides
in every smallest thing—
bracket of a petal,
facet of a stone,
a raindrop's sliding
spring
from one new leaf,
translated as
the shaken
shadow
of a wing—

THE BIRD-SERMON

He reached a place called Bevagna, in which a great multitude of birds of different kinds had gathered ... and ran swiftly towards them, leaving his companions on the road. When he got very close, seeing that they were waiting for him, he greeted them in his usual way. He was quite surprised, however, because the birds did not fly away, as they usually do. Filled with great joy, he humbly requested them to listen to the word of God. Among many other things, he said to them: 'My brother birds, you should praise your Creator greatly, and love Him always ...'

Celano, Life 1, xxi

After the Crucifixion Triptych in the Courtauld Gallery

You preached by starlight to night birds.
A dozen came. They perched along
the gilded branches of a tree
like jeweller's stock. Fire-speckled larks,

blue-throated sparrows, thrushes cloaked
in silver beads, hoopoes whose crests
stood spined in gold. Fine fowls, all these:
their gaze as much upon themselves

as you. Your tired companion slept
under a chasuble of stars,
hand propping cheek. But you, fired up,
awake to God, preached on and on.

They did not stir. Perhaps each phrase
slid off their smooth enamelled backs
like rain, like light. Yet on one limb
set separately the wisest bird,
wide-eyed and cowled, weighed every word.

Marine Parade, Brighton

First dawn, December. Random gulls adrift
aimless above the sea and the coast road,
sliding their long descent or longer lift
into dissolving parallels of cloud,

grey upon grey. A teenage boy, unsteady
from the night before, comes loping slow
along the promenade. His bin-bag's heavy,
crammed full of bread. Already in the know

gulls skirl down shrieking. Rough-torn chunks hurled out
stick in their throats, gag, choke them, till they flop
sated away, splay-legged, while losers shout
lasting revenge. Then, bright, the boy flings up

in high parabolas small teasing crumbs
the breeze takes, and the breeze-tossed birds gulp in
beakfuls that seem instructive; for they come
humbly to earth, lined up beside the bin

and on the rails, in ruffled order spaced
wing's-widths apart: each waiting for its turn
to snatch a portion of allotted grace,
to eat and learn.

A starling
murmuration
scythes the cold sky,
pours out like grain:
form audible,
prayer
visible

SISTERS

One day he came to a village called Alviano to preach ... and
called for silence. But a large number of swallows nesting there
were shrieking and chirping. Since he could not be heard by the
people, he said to the noisy birds: 'My sister swallows, now it is
time for me to speak, since you have already said enough ...'

Celano, *Life* 1, xxi

He ordered the Brothers to avoid completely honeyed poison, that
is, familiarity with women ... Indeed, the female troubled him
so much that you would believe this was neither caution nor good
example, but fear or terror ... When he preached to them, he
would not look them in the face ... He said it was not safe.

Celano, *Remembrance of the Desire of a Soul* 1, lxxviii, lxxx;
Bonaventure, *Life*, v, 5

[When he preached to the Ladies, as he called them, who were
with Clare at San Damiano] he raised his eyes to heaven and
began to pray to Christ. Then he had ashes brought and made a
circle with them round himself on the floor, then put the rest on
his own head. As the ladies waited, he remained silent within
the circle of ashes, and real amazement grew in their hearts.
Suddenly he got up and, to their great surprise, recited the 'Have
mercy on me, God', instead of a sermon. Then he left, fast.

Celano, *Remembrance of the Desire of a Soul* 1, clvii

As you begin to preach
                swallows from tower and thatch
sweep the exuberant sky,
                white-bodiced arrow-screams
joying to chase and snatch
                existence on the fly,
but not your words or dreams—

As you begin to sing
                cicadas in the trees,
sisters with fret-saw wings,
                rasp shrill and shrill and shrill
noonday's eternities
                in sun-and-shadow hymns
from thicket and from hill—

As you begin to pray
                the Ladies in surmise
raise their veiled heads, pink mouths
                murmuring for holy bread,
with unaverted eyes
                as doves in restless crowds,
or babies to be fed—

their forms as one inclined
                to you, their heaven-carrier,

and your swift-blessing hand—
        while you, too far entwined,
heap up your fool's-ash barrier,
        inviolable land.

Against the heaving roller-coaster sea,
in-rushing with its whale-back curves, shot-grey
and thundering, riffed through with wind-chased
scatterings of foam, two girls audaciously
bunch up their skirts to trudge their arduous way
through shingle to the edge. There, swaying-braced,

gripping each other, neither rightly hears
the roaring admonitions of the waves,
for they can sing as loud. Stuck chanting there
they pull their fashion hats across their ears,
lift up their phones—and while the water raves,
uselessly tidy their escaping hair.

From behind
their revolving hatch
of silence,
nuns feed
the town
with holiness
twice baked,
fresh-sugared

THE CROWD

On May 8th 1213 Francis preached in a packed palace courtyard before Count Orlando of Chiusi de La Verna, beginning his sermon with the words of a troubadour's song:

> *'So great the joy I have in sight*
> *That every pain I count delight.'*
>
> Fioretti, First Consideration of the Stigmata

As he preached he moved his feet as if he was dancing ... not playfully, but burning with the fire of divine love.

Celano, *Life* 1, xxvii

At Bologna he preached in the Piazza before the Palazzo Publico, where almost the whole town was assembled. The theme of his sermon was 'Angels, men, devils' ... The people's reverence and devotion towards him was so great ... that men and women rushed upon him headlong, anxious to touch the hem of his garment and carry away bits of his clothing.

Thomas of Spalato, a student eyewitness
in 1222 *(New Fioretti, p. 63)*

You are the preacher; you are the toast of the fair.
Francis the saviour, Francis with ash in his hair,
you in your rags and renouncings, with shins chicken-bare,
whom cripples creep after, whom babes-in-arms hold in a
    stare—
whom worldlings crush close for a kiss of your hand, for
    a prayer.

You tell of great angels you've met as you travel the land,
so lithe in their quicksilver mercies, so stern in command;
tell of the rolling-eyed bristling devils who stand
at the beds of the dying, as plain as your arm or your
    hand,
clanking iron buckets to capture fresh souls if they can—

but everyone's saved by the gift that is Jesus the King's,
worth more than castles, bay horses, stiff linen, gold rings;
grace earned by knot-cords and Poverty, fasting and
    hymns,
by weeping the snow-flood repentance of Apennine springs—
and as they weep with you, from somewhere a troubadour
    sings.

Love is his theme, but as found in poetical books,
not bleeding and dying for sinners on butchering hooks;
Heaven's his goal, but not God's, in whose emerald bower
Death like a snake sags and dies, disembowelled of its
    power;

joy brims him full, but not yours, as with road-callused feet
you dance your high ecstasy there in the throng of the
    street,
under the stars whose brass circuits revolve now and ring
descants to each word you say, every note that you sing.

Mornington Crescent, London, December

Out of the station dancing he weaves his way,
snapping his fingers, jigging, on drugs perhaps,
while those of us working, purposeful, faces grey,
pass in our armour of mobiles and coffee cups—
as he spirals into the bus lane, laughing loud
at his skill to make taxis hoot and cyclists swear,
dancing the unthought and the not-allowed,
flaunting his verve and folly and shaking hair—
and the sun comes up on the Crescent, urban, wan,
just-there, in the midst of the whirling and shouts and
    shooing,
and he stops to salute with a higher, wilder song
its wonder-and-splendour rising, all his doing.

Wind-blown,
the blare
of joyous
brass
redoubles
the silence
of the hills

DEUS MEUS ET OMNIA

[When he stayed once with Bernard of Quintavalle, then a rich layman of Assisi, who later became his first follower], Bernard set it in his heart to watch his sanctity, wherefore he made ready for him a bed in his own chamber ... And when Francis thought that Bernard was asleep ... he rose from his bed and set himself to pray. And with exceeding great fervour, lifting up his hands and raising his eyes to heaven, he said: 'My God and my all! Deus meus et omnia!' And thus saying and sorely weeping he stayed till morning, always repeating: 'My God and my all!'

Fioretti, i

'All a Brother needs is the Pater Noster.'

Francis in *Verba Conradi (New Fioretti, p.39)*

'The only thing we may glory in is our infirmities.'

Francis, *First Rule*

All night you ward off sleep
as in a joust,
rigid in linen sheets
and in disgust
that they should feast and spoil you,
a thing of dust.

You should be in the woods
on iron-hard ground,
under His lancing stars
frost-limbed, frost-bound
to feel His pattern through you,
His grip around.

Suppose that He should come
and find you here,
a simpleton in pillows
smoothed ear to ear,
with balm that is His portion
stroked in your hair.

You need no more than this
bare wall, bare floor
and whipping cord to slay
what you long for.
You long for Him. Beside Him,
nothing more.

Youngest by thirty years among the priests
he kneels down swiftly, neatly, and must lift
the heavy monstrance in his blushing hands,
secure, not shaking, under such a gift—

The Adoration over, he is found
shyly beside the door, while spinsters press
twittering around him, to observe up close
his fresh and unexpected holiness.

Reed-thin, he fingers one small sausage roll,
smilingly turning down all other food—
for he must ride his borrowed bicycle
back to some terrace off the Cowley Road,

where in his darkened flat he'll slide alone
into the narrow sheet-cell of his bed,
holding his kitten in his praying hands.
She is pure white. He has not named her yet.

OBLATION

THE TREE-CROSS

By 1220, the Order numbered around 1,000 Brothers. Many were sent on missions abroad.

Wherever [he and the Brothers] saw a cross or the sign of a cross, whether on the ground, on a wall, in trees or in roadside hedges, they would prostrate themselves on the ground, saying 'We adore you O Christ ... and we bless You, because by Your Holy Cross You have redeemed the world.'

Celano *Life* 1, xvii

Is it any wonder that the wondrous Cross, taking root inside him, and sprouting in such good soil, should bear such remarkable flowers, leaves and fruit? That wonderful Cross from the beginning claimed him entirely for itself.

Celano, *Remembrance of the Desire of a Soul* 2, lxxv

From the tightening of his nerves [with suffering] his limbs became rigid, like those of a dead man.

Letter of Brother Elias *(New Fioretti*, p. 81)

The seedling grew
as in the margin
of a book.

The shoot
disturbed you sometimes;
Brothers
scratched your back
for fleas.

The branches
stiffened your veins
to taut
strings—

into the singing
semblance
of His Cross

Crux fidelis, inter omnes
arbor una nobilis;
nulla talem silva profert,
flore, fronde, germine.
Dulce lignum, dulce clave,
dulce pondens sustinens!

Faithful Cross! Above all other
one and only noble Tree!
none in foliage, none in blossom,
none in fruit thy peer may be,
sweetest wood and sweetest iron,
sweetest weight is hung on thee!

Venantius Fortunatus, 6ᵗʰ century

Lone
lean
questioning
thorn,
worm-
mazed
or
pierced
with
light

CALL AND REPLY

He remained a long time in his place of prayer, frequently repeating the phrase: 'Lord, be merciful to me, a sinner.' Or, 'Most sweet Lord, I long to love Thee.' ... He prayed unceasingly until he sensed he had been heard.

Celano, *Life* 1, ix, *Remembrance of the Desire of a Soul* 2, xvii;
Bartholemew of Pisa (*New Fioretti*, pp. 61–2)

'Disturbed once at prayer, he came out excitedly shouting "What's all this! What's all this?".... [On another occasion], asking himself why the world ran after him, he cried: "Why after me? Why after me?"'

Bologna MS (*New Fioretti*, p. 53); *Fioretti*, ix

[In the 13th year of his conversion he journeyed to Syria, where long and bitter battles were being waged daily between Christians and pagans.] He was not afraid to present himself to the sight of the Sultan of the Saracens ... speaking with eloquence and confidence ... and the Sultan was moved by his words.

Celano, *Life* 1, xx

[When he was making the new Rule] the voice of Christ was heard in the air, answering Francis's cry, 'Lord, did I not tell You that they would not believe You?' Christ said: 'I want the Rule to be observed as it is to the letter, to the letter, to the letter, and without a gloss, and without a gloss, and without a gloss.' Then Francis turned to the Brothers and said: 'Do you hear? Do you hear? Would you like me to have it said to you again?'

Mirror of Perfection, 1

Your cry so plaintive, like a gull's
blown on the gale, repeatedly
the what and why and how of it,
present, and past, and what's to be,
querying, seeking, pressing, through
the wide God-line of hills or sea—

Your cry aboard that eggshell boat
rocking towards the pagan's lair,
'Soldan!' among his tents of war,
a hooded falcon by his ear
that mews of Christ, and Christ, and Christ,
to make him hear—to make him hear—

Down Umbrian roads your throbbing call,
'Humility!' a rock-dove's sighs
out of the woods, and 'Poverty!',
a curlew's keening fall and rise
over the waste, where Brothers walk
with your hard lessons in their eyes—

Then 'To the letter! Without gloss!'
Christ's magpie and his clerking-bird,
warning beak open—yet most days,
far off within the holm-oak wood
you are that unseen chorister
who cries My God, my God, my God.

Kingston near Lewes, East Sussex, March

On the churned muddy field below the hill
four boys are playing football, and their shrill
cries of 'Man on!', 'Mine!', 'Leave it!', 'Goal!'
tangle and mingle in the evening chill;

but as the lid of night begins to fall
making a moon-ghost of the curving ball,
it seems their only contest is to call
and draw an answer, or no word at all.

Smooth master
of his clarinet,
a blackbird sings
from some far tree;
the one who answers,
farther yet,
knows no such rain-pure
minstrelsy,
but mimics him
as best it can—
thus bare
to Godhead
warbles man

NAKEDNESS

[Having asked Brother Rufino 'by Holy Obedience' to preach half-naked in Assisi, he rebuked himself severely, and climbed completely naked into the pulpit to preach the nakedness and shame of the Passion of Christ. ...]

Fioretti xxix, excerpted

On many occasions, when the poor approached him, he would spontaneously give them his mantle, his tunic or even his trousers. The Brothers sometimes tried to stop these donations ...

Celano, *Remembrance of the Desire of a Soul 2*, liii–lix

Once, walking along a road in a biting wind, he felt himself becoming faint-hearted. So he summoned up his courage and, climbing a hill, took off his clothes and turned to face the wind. Then he told himself that it would be good to have even one tunic.

Brother Ralph of Rheims *(New Fioretti, p. 42)*

'Brothers must expose themselves to all things.'

Francis, *First Rule*

To cast the casing is the thing.
To peel in one swift spiralling
skin from an onion; crack the nut
to get the meat and goodness out;
whittle the wood. And scrabble off
all your concealing over-stuff—

All poor and shuddering souls may take
your clothes away, for Jesus's sake;
any who suffer, starved or hurt,
can have your ragged undershirt—
yes, even tear your fraying sleeve
for shreds of grace, as they believe.

No need for tunic, cloak or drawers,
all that is falsely labelled yours—
This is your body, white and spare,
tensing and scrawny; here's the air.
Naked, you are His child indeed,
uncovered, unadorned and freed—
nothing but flesh, bone, blood and hairs,
elation,
tears.

Hove beach, early March

Shoes off and socks off, with his milk-white feet
absurdly fragile, somehow incomplete,
the wary human, high-arched, muscles curled,
steps out towards the new rim of the world.

It's not as he expected it. The sand
hard-packed and cold, the wide pale lip of land
licked and licked over by the tumbling sea
with famished and with grinding urgency.

But freedom swells with every gulp of air:
spirit unfettered, out-of-season bare
in Nature. Treasure-stones entice and flash
purely for him. And now he will enmesh

his essence with the sea: stretch, paddle, dance,
make yogic gym-club forms. The sea, askance,
scorns him, as all that's done along its shores;
but vastly, in its inmost veins, applauds.

Each stripping-off
brings beauty out—
so twining brambles
winter-red
vault now and shine,
as in proud leaf
they'd never do

ROSES

'Each of us has his enemy in his power—that is, the body by which he sins. The body is ever at variance with all that is good.'

Francis, *First Rule*

He and his Brothers did not hesitate, if troubled by burning of the flesh, to cover themselves in blood from gashing their bodies with sharp thorns.

Celano, *Life* 1, xv

Troubled once by sinful thoughts, he threw himself into a thorn hedge. It flowered into deep-pink thornless roses (*canina Assisiensis*) which grow only in a small garden beside Sta Maria dei Angeli, or the Portiuncula.

A fresco by Giotto at Assisi shows Holy Poverty, at her marriage to Francis, in rags and with her feet torn by thorns; but she is crowned with light and rose-sprays.

Rose garden, Sta Maria dei Angeli

Now, as a last resort, the thorns.
The quickset hedge. It throws you off,
but you force in, to lacerate
all that can gape and bleed enough.
How that red flows, while you, impaled
like galls, like vermin, wish the pain
to mount, mount more, be His. At last
insensibility sets in.
Bone weariness. Damp freshening leaves
weave up your wounds. The mountain elm
showers its white petals over you.
And then, without a shield or helm,
cleansed as a knight who's hacked his way
remorseless through the sweetbriar wood,
you gain your prize of roses turned
thornless as grass or gratitude;
crimsoning as pricked-finger blood.

Rose garden, Romney Marsh

Low-laughing the roses were gone again,
tumbling their petals over the garden wall,
whispering silken summer, but in moments
fled far beyond recall—

From doorway and from casement disappearing,
leaving behind unfilled, ungathered air
empty of sway and sweetness, as if fearing
ever to settle there.

All metaphors and similes evading,
velvet or satin, colours of fire or dawn,
from every hedge and border swiftly fading
to dream, as dew from lawn,

from web, from spray. No adjectives can frame them,
nor any grid of poetry or prose;
we catch their beauty only as we name them,
rose, rose.

The wild white rose
survives
the scattering wind,
but not the hand
that seeks
so tenderly
to touch it,
bring it
close

JESUS

For him the Nativity was the feast of feasts, when God was made a little child and hung upon human breasts ... The melting compassion of his heart towards the Child Jesus made him stammer sweet words as babies do. This name was to him like honey and honeycomb in his mouth.

Celano, *Remembrance of the Desire of a Soul* 2, cli

Daily, constantly, talk of Jesus was always on his lips. He was always with Jesus ... Jesus in his heart, Jesus in his mouth, Jesus in his ears, Jesus in his eyes, Jesus in his hands ... Often he sat down to dinner but on saying, or hearing, or even thinking 'Jesus', he forgot bodily food.

Celano, *Life* 2, ix

The holy honeycomb
of 'I' and 'H' and 'S'
fragments within your mouth,
flows into sacredness.

That tiny baby-sigh,
the gentle Virgin's first
mother-and-milk embrace,
breathes from you kissed and nursed,

lip-sweetening holy Name
too heart-held to be heard,
too dear to stammer out,
that radiant lovely Word,

savoured upon the tongue
confided to the cheek,
until when left alone
you kneel again to speak

those syllables to silence
beside the empty board:
no sustenance but this,
Jesus, my Jesus, Lord.

Laden with beer cans, Finals-light, they cram
the table-seating in the Brighton train.
It's Friday night. It's June. The girl in green,
squeezed into it, white tattooed arms not yet
browned by the sun, has just completely nailed
the Hegel paper; it's like, Oh my God,
she wrote six fucking sides! Jesus, how good
was that? Her neighbour, leather-clad and trans,
hair in a raven bouffant, proudly shares
his student profile: 'Guys, I said I was
a penguin living in Antarctica.'
Hooting, they drink to boldness. Well, why not
invent a profile, take a name in vain;
who will defend, restore it? Maybe names
will do it by themselves; allow their weight
to float in slowly, slowly as the moon
that swims in view outside the window-glass,
huge-blown with summer, pink and misty-veiled
above the approaching city; and they fall
silent at sight of it, till one remarks
into the dark, 'Jesus, that's beautiful.'

Tingle
of
the loved name
spoken—
a smile
that
hesitates
to break

TASTES OF MANNA

When he was called to a dinner given by great princes ... he would taste some meat in order to observe the Holy Gospel. The rest, which he appeared to eat, he put in his lap ... or down the neck of his habit ...

Celano, *Life* 1, xix

He always sought out a hidden place where he could join to God not only his spirit but every member of his body. When it happened that he was suddenly overcome in public by a visitation of the Lord, so as not to be without a cell he would make a little cell out of his mantle. Sometimes when he had no mantle, he would cover his face with his sleeve to avoid revealing the hidden manna.... Even on the road, with his companions going on ahead, he would stop in his tracks ...

Celano, *Remembrance of the Desire of a Soul* 2, lxi

Their meals you did not eat. You chewed
the meat a little, crumbled paste
to pieces, blushing to seem rude
or graceless, or in too much haste;
then like some drab brown mother-bird
close-gorging chicks within the nest,
you with a silent spit transferred
to hood or sleeve the half-pulped mess,
so no one saw...

                  So no one saw,
you rode through Borgo with that sleeve
crust-sour across your face, to feel
His secret feeding; there receive
as from a soft-bowed phrase, or small
child's trusting touch, or butterfly
that lights upon you, tenderness
you dare not grasp, in case you die
in that chance time, that sudden place.

Sometimes we are allowed to parry it.
We put up hands against the red
concerto of a winter sky, the dim-
starred honey-drift of jasmine flowers, a run
of five heart-hushing notes, and they comply,
stirring yet not translating us. But then
it waits in ambush, this unnamed, unknown,
to strike us as we hard-shove cases up
into the overhead compartment, or
pull out a drawer to find a pair of socks,
or stand defenceless at a counter, poised
to ask for the manchego—then it comes,
that all-dissolving sweetness, sweeping through
until we have no spine to stand, no weight
with which we can resist—

                      while all around
the world goes on: scales, bank-card, plastic bag,
clang of the opening door (that opening door
so dangerous now, a floodgate into love
out of the rapids of the surging street)—
But all goes on. It is not rearranged.
Perfectly normal. Just as we'd expect.

On the milk-blue
stilling
evening sea
the sun
sets a boat,
just one,
aflame

DEMONS

When he slept with a feather pillow given to him by John of Greccio, he slept so badly— 'as if I'd eaten bread with darnel in it' —that he believed the Devil was in the pillow, and threw it away . . .

Scripta Leonis, 94

When he was staying with the Cardinal of Santa Croce in Rome, demons came and fiercely attacked him when he was trying to sleep . . . They beat him long and hard, and left him half-dead . . . trembling and quaking in every limb. He said they had done it because he was setting a bad example by staying in palaces . . . 'Demons', he said, 'are God's castaldi *[police].'*

Celano, *Remembrance of the Desire of a Soul* 2, lxxxiv

The Devil called to him, 'Francis! Francis! Francis!' And he answered, 'What do you want?'

Ibid., lxxxi

A thistle prick inside a shoe
halts you. The rustle of a leaf
must give you pause. Chatter of stars
alerts you, and the spit of rain.
Chastisings fill the air again.

Francis! each one calls out to you,
Francis! to make you turn and look,
disrupting prayer—but curbing, too,
delicate eating, or desire
to linger long beside the fire.

So when plush pillows jump with knives,
or shadows punch you senseless; when
kicks break your ribs, and bloody teeth
scream out your name, you fight—until
He whispers this is not His will.

On the Brighton–London train, early morning

To each incessant flicking
of his phone
he bobs his head,
a nervous bird, quick-pecking
seed fresh-sown,
or crumbs of bread;
with each nod disengaging
from domains
considered real,
that multimedia staging
by the dawn,
bare woods, glass, steel;
with each twitch tighter captured
in soft seines
spread whim to whim,
while he, enwrapt, enraptured,
silent lets
them smother him.

Nettle-touches
not unfriendly
by the gatepost,
in the orchard—
silken
spite

APPLES

'One of the ways the Devil will try to destroy the Order will be through bad and thoughtless admissions. Evil spirits will make all kinds of unsuitable men want to join.'

Francis in *Angelo Clareno, Expositio Regulae*
(New Fioretti, p. 30)

'Understand this about what is going to happen. In the beginning of our way of life together we will find fruit that is very sweet and nice. A little later, fruit that is not so pleasant and sweet will be served. Finally fruit will be served that is full of bitterness ... Although it will look fine and fragrant on the surface, it will be too sour for anyone to eat.'

Francis in Celano, *Life* 1, xi

Leo recounted that at one point Francis arose from prayer in great spiritual distress, and did not want to have an Order any more. Then Brother Masseo went to him and said, 'Have you never seen an apple all rotten on the surface, but when you cut it open you may find, inside, that the heart is good?' And Francis said, 'Yes, you're right ... More good than bad!'

Bartholemew of Pisa *(New Fioretti*, p. 86)

Perfection grows on apple trees.
In dream you walk beneath the boughs
gathering red and gold to fill
a bag, like stars. The sky broods dark,
the leaves moss-grey, in silence. Prayer
dews every blade of bending grass.
You pick the fruit for saving souls,
heavy with goodness and with light.

The trees are countless, though. By scores
they mist away. Your weakening eyes
will never see them all. On rocks
and stony slopes they're thin, diseased.
Your Gospel splints won't hold them up;
your words won't swell these tiny fruits,
acidic in your puckering mouth
as winter sloes. You walk no more.

Your star-filled scrip deceives you, too.
Shiny has soured to tarnish; firm
proves spongy-rotten when you press;
maggots squirm through. Ripe red twists round
to callow green. And yet, that said,
on this storm-splintered branch hangs one
wrinkled and shrunken, starling-pecked,
which slices white—and then exudes
the scent of the Beatitudes.

Information for exhibitors at the East Dean and Friston Show

Beans: straight and young.
Cabbage: solid heart.
Lettuce: well washed,
          crisp and tender,
          with firm hearts,
          and roots intact.
Parsnips: straight, well-shouldered,
          with skin
          free of blemishes.
Apples and pears: should be shown
          with stalks attached,
          and the fruit
          must never be polished.

          The maximum number
          of points awarded
          is governed by
          the degree of difficulty
          of producing
          a perfect
          exhibit

Five baskets left
beneath an apple tree
on which
few fruits remain:
a rough-weave convocation
loitering,
unheeding
of the rain

WATER

'Laudato si, mi Signore, per sor' Acqua,
la quale e molto utile et humile et pretiosa et casta.
*Be praised, My Lord, for Sister Water, who is most useful, and
humble, and lovely, and chaste.'*

Francis, *Canticle of Brother Sun*

*When he washed his hands, he chose a place where the washing
water would not be trampled underfoot.*

Scripta Leonis, 51

*When he stayed at the Eremo di Montecasale, Francis would
drink only water from the natural rock spring above the stream,
not from the interior well.*

Guide to the Hermitage

*One day ... when it was raining constantly he got off his horse
to say the Office, and standing for a while he got completely
soaked.*

Celano, *Remembrance of the Desire of a Soul* 1, lxii

Across the path
Water has spread
her robes of silk,
her braids of glass.
Agimus tibi
gratias.

Within the well
Water awaits
in moss-smoothed depths
of sunken sky,
immutable,
content to lie.

Caught from the rock
Water runs through
your beard, your hair,
too joyously
to linger there,
but glittering, free,

scatters herself,
for in her truth
to be made whole
is to be torn
wholly apart,
poured out, reborn.

Roadside spring, Powys

My water's in a bottle, but just here
is water from the rock. It trickles down
invisible through fern and bramble, clear
flow-song materialising on wet stone,
as if at some command. No, summer's grass
did not request it, nor the damsel flies
mesmerised blue, nor stone-eyed sheep that press
beside the wall; nor I. But, lent this prize,
I pass my finger carefully through heart-
and breath-suspending cold; then, tentative,
I raise some to my lips, which will not part
to taste it, though by drinking I might live
as angels do, or gods—

                              I should leave now,
except, to prove I have not failed that test,
I swiftly sign a little to my brow
and wander on, approved, light-headed, blessed.

Soaked through,
the meadow
gives itself to prayer
in rain-gorged clover, sorrel, feather grass;
or as the drooping plantain head
rough-brown and tonsured round with silver drops
bowed forward, forward more
under this sweetness

THE VIRGIN OF THE FISHES

Francis spent one Lent in solitude on Isola Maggiore in Lake Trasimeno. His only shelter was a thicket of bushes; his only food was two small loaves, and when he was fetched after forty days he had eaten only half of one of them.

Fioretti vi, excerpted

When he had a chance he would throw back into the water live fish that had been caught, and he warned them to be careful not to be caught again. Once when he was sitting in a little boat at the port on Lake Rieti, a fisherman caught a large tench and reverently offered it to him. He accepted it gladly and gratefully, calling it 'Brother'. He put it back in the water next to the little boat, and with devotion blessed the name of the Lord. For some time that fish did not leave the spot, playing in the water where he put it ...

Celano, *Life* 1, xxi

Blue lies the lake. Blue folded lie
the misted mountains and the sky;
the Virgin's cloak envelops you.
Her beauty is diffused in blue.

Frail stars of blackthorn overhead
shelter your shivering Lenten bed;
but Her night mantle, draping low,
drops down fire-stars upon the snow.

In that containment nothing's heard
save lap of water or of bird,
while Virgin-serving angels lace
above the lake their nets of grace,

and rescued fish, their gills prised free
from hook and bait, mill in that sea
to mouth a silent antiphon,
blue sequins swarming to the moon.

Brighton, shortest day

Slow through the selvedges of day and night,
lit stem to stern, two fishing vessels ply
between the sandbanks of the sea and sky

towards the evening star, which shines and hangs
as on the shore of their remotest thought,
waiting to catch them, or itself be caught.

Half-anchored
on beach-grass,
a tiny
coiled
snail
awaits
the next
perilous
updraught of air

TO THE SUMMIT

He tended to flee human company and go off to the most remote places, so that, letting go of every care, only the wall of the flesh would stand between him and God.

Celano, *Life* 2, vi

Wherever he stayed for prayer he wished to be remote enough for no one to go to him unless he called him.

Scripta Leonis, 31

To climb until you know the place;
until the piled rocks sing a word
you have not said,
they have not heard.

To climb till no one finds your trace,
leaving your love to keep them all,
whispering to Him,
Be merciful.

To climb until you know the place:
your breath a labour in the air
and water, wolf
unsighted there.

To climb till no one finds your trace,
by yellow broom, on slipping stone,
where you have passed
and wept alone.

To climb until you know the place:
brushed by the hem of God, who fills
the sounding bowl
of circled hills.

Beachy Head, East Sussex

There is no point except the very edge,
the utmost brink, though it may murder us
as it has murdered others. On this ledge
lie still-wrapped wilted flowers, each makeshift cross

black at the skyline. Rising ravens cough
a brief condolence. But there is no point
except the edge, that dare of tipping off
to nothingness, or where the ravens went,

staggering, wind-borne. So the bold sightseer
shrugs off his back-pack, keeping just his phone;
lightens himself, though white chalk shoots down sheer
to the beach where a man, small as a stone,

calls his dog faintly from infinity—
Here is the very place, exactly here,
where he will smile
                        into the lens
                                    and see

CONSUMMATION

LARKS

'Sister Lark has a hood like a nun and is a humble bird, who goes cheerfully along the road to find herself some corn; and even if she finds it in animal dung she takes it out and eats it. As she flies she praises God, like a good religious despising earthly things, for her life is always in the heavens. Moreover her clothing is made like the earth—her feathers, that is—giving an example to religious that they ought not to have gaudy and fancy clothing but soil-coloured, as if they were dead.'

Francis in *Scripta Leonis*, 110

'Laudato si, mi Signore, per frate Vento,
et per aere et nubilo et sereno....
Praise to you, my Lord, for Brother Wind, and for the air and the clouds and the blue sky.'

Francis, *Canticle of Brother Sun*

You who would give your limbs, your life
for this, for this,
run in the fields and clap and call
out of their bliss
little larks fluttering, whirring-winged
up towards Him,
leaping in trills of prayer, until
skies blur, eyes dim—
trespassing where the angels glide,
swift to prepare
grace-notes and sparks of chastening fire
out of pure air;
flickering close to heavenly halls
where soon, you trust,
billowing wide your sleeves, your wings,
you'll lose the dust—
springing like them from mud, from slime,
to quit the earth,
soaring from dunghill scavenging
towards rebirth;
hooded and humble, poor and mean,
the larks and you,
God's minstrel too.

Wolstonbury Hill, May

To step on skylarks—
       easy
as treading on earth,
brown hectic specks
muddling up,
and up, and up,
wings scissor-touching,
muted with fright—

Then, out of sight,
a throb in the stretched drum
       over the sea,
curling faint down
that song, saying never
never to be found
the nest—unless
it is this hollow here,
holding in thin straw
shell-scraps of sky

What do they sing
            over frost-savaged grass
at the first of the spring,
            to rough sheep clustering
in a wind
      keen as glass?

  O Claritas!

BECOMING LIGHT

*One day, marvelling at the Lord's mercy, he began to lose himself;
his feelings were pressed together; and that darkness disappeared
which fear of sin had gathered in his heart ... Then he was
caught up above himself and totally engulfed in light.*

Celano, *Life* 1, xi

*One Lent he had been making a small cup, so as not to waste
any spare time. But one day as he was devoutly saying terce, his
eyes casually fell on the cup ... and he felt his inner self was
being hindered in its devotion ... So he grabbed the cup and
burned it in the fire.*

Celano, *Remembrance of the Desire of a Soul* 2, lxiii

'*A servant of God should be burning with life and holiness so
brightly that by the light of example ... he will rebuke all the
wicked.*'

Francis in Celano, Ibid., lxix

That day when you became desire—
That time when you were snatched entire
into His Light, and loving fled
out of yourself, one flame from heart
through parting skull—for moments then
you were that silly wooden cup
you'd made in Lent, its burnished lip
glossed acorn-brown, which, glimpsed again
(distracting thing, so fondly carved
for foolish hours) you flung instead
instant from lower into higher:
instant into unmaking fire.

St Andrew's Church, Bishopstone, East Sussex

Crop-haired, a little lame,
she polishes the church
on Saturdays, her turn;
always the shuffling same
hoovering of the nave,
the dusting of the pews
(though dust is rare, she says)
with flowers to change or save;
and if she should feel low
she leans a little while
against the wall where glass
throws on its opal glow—
and is transfigured so.

Mid-winter morning:
figures freeze
in nimbus breath,
their dogs the same.
Tumultuous grass
a frost-fire sea;
the spangled path
not stones
but stars

FIRE

'Laudato si, mi Signore, per frate Focu,
Per lo quale ennallumini la nocte;
Ed ello e bello et iucundo et robustoso et forte.
Praise to you, my Lord, for Brother Fire, by which we light up
the night; and he is beautiful and cheerful and vigorous and
strong.'

Francis, Canticle of Brother Sun

He loved and respected fire with such charity and attention, and
took so much joy in it ... that if anyone did not treat it properly,
he was upset. He chatted to fire with inward and outward joy,
just as if it felt, understood and could talk about God ...

Scripta Leonis, 49

'My Brother Fire, your beauty is the envy of all creatures ... Be
gracious to me in this hour! Be courteous! For a long time I have
loved you in the Lord. I pray the great Lord who created you to
temper now your heat ...'

Francis, when about to be cauterised for eye
disease. Celano, Life 2, cxxv

He spared lanterns, lamps and candles, unwilling to use his hand
to put out their brightness, which is a sign of the Eternal Light.

Celano, Remembrance of the Desire of a Soul 2, cxxiv

You begged courtesy of Fire—
asked him to doff
his flaring cap to you,
hold slightly off
his scorching robe, and bow
quivering before you,
as he knows how.

You sought comity with Fire—
hoped he would share
his beauty, which is God's;
toss his gold hair
and teach you his high song
whistling with Heaven-light,
to sing along.

You begged graciousness of Fire—
asked him to shed
his sparking spurs at least
before his tread
seared you; and put away
his swift soft razors
for another day.

Yet knowing his high nature
you did not require
Eternal Light to spare you
in form of Fire;
but, open-armed and meek,
bent to His kiss
licked through your cheek.

The wick dug deep in hardened wax
at first rebuffs the playful match,
won't rise to it, but keeps itself

even from breath of it, as if
it's made of some impervious stuff,
fire-ignorant. A second touch

and it relents, combusting now
to smoulder-blue and to one least
live orange fibre of desire,

a stamen only. In its pool
of warming oil it hesitates,
flicked by this brightness—nudged until

it sinks with one last golden tame
flower of surrender, perfect flame.

In white ash
marrowed
lava-red
one
cleft green
pear-wood branch
remains,
sweet-misting
evening

THE HERB GARDEN

He ordered the gardener to set aside within the garden a smaller enclosure for aromatic and flowering herbs, so that those who saw them might recall the memory of Eternal Savour.

Celano, *Remembrance of the Desire of a Soul* 2, cxxiv

The Brothers often urged him to give some relief to his frail and weakened body with the help of doctors. But he absolutely refused to do this ... So God multiplied His mercy in him, and he contracted a serious disease of the eyes. Day after day the disease grew worse, and seemed to be aggravated daily from lack of treatment ... [Eventually, he was completely blind.]

Celano, *Life* 2, iv

At the time of his last illness, and in the dark of night, he wanted to eat some parsley and humbly asked for it. The cook was called, but complained: 'I've been picking parsley every day, and I've cut off so much of it that even in broad daylight I can hardly find any. Even more so now that darkness has fallen; I won't be able to distinguish it from the other herbs.' 'Brother,' the saint replied, 'don't worry; bring me the first herbs your hand touches.' ... And when he brought them, there was a leafy, tender stem of parsley right in the middle.

Celano, *Remembrance of the Desire of a Soul* 2, xxii

By the night window you breathe deep.
You know He has been walking here.
His footsteps have made drunk the grass;
He's breezed among blue lavender,
dreamed by the curling camomile,
on grey sage smudged His silken hair;
grasped spitefulness of rosemary
whose grieving fumigates the air,
and has plucked out, to test it true,
the spare frail parsley that is you.

Borgo di Vagli, Umbria

As pale as April, petalled rosemary
mirrors the sky, and blundering bees career
in gliding spirals, carried giddily
on promises of aromatic air.

In August both have vanished, long-dead flowers
fallen to earth, and languorous needle-spikes
infused for sand-slow, lizard-flickered hours
in steeping sun; but as this still-warm night

wraps the bush round, a luminous chill glow
betrays the mystery that's nested there:
a worm or pulsing worm-soul, zenith-blue
as in their April day the blossoms were.

Entraced
in thyme,
wings
sapphire-still,
the butterfly
consents to stay—
can't break
away

BIRD-SOULS

*Once, when he was crossing the Lake of Rieti, a fisherman offered
him a little water-bird so that he might rejoice in the Lord over
it. He received it gladly, with open hands, and invited it to fly
away freely. But the bird did not want to leave; instead it settled
in his hands as if in a nest, and he remained in prayer ...*

Celano, *Remembrance of the Desire of a Soul* 2, cxxvi

*When he preached to them, the birds rejoiced in a wonderful way
... They stretched their necks, spread their wings, opened their
beaks, and gazed at him. He passed through them, touching their
heads and bodies with his tunic. Then he blessed them ... and
gave them permission to fly off to another place.*

Celano, *Life* 1, xxi

A water bird, he says it is,
as he draws on
his slapping oar to get across
before day's gone;
a water bird, light as a shell,
whose rainbow sheen
breathes Heaven underneath your hand,
intact, serene;
a water bird whose opaque eye
half-closed in sleep
contains this lake, this mountainside,
snowed height, black deep.
Trembling you guard this being now,
warm as a coal,
just-held, as by the dipping prow
your life: your soul.

Council garden, North London

The sick dove by the hedge
the thrush beside the fence
quiveringly challenge
our indifference—

We want to save them,
but are uncertain how—
long to lift them gently
to the here and now,

yet passing later
we part-understand:
shunning the clumsiness
of human hand,

they've stretched their necks,
spread out their wings;
not dying, flying
past the end of things.

Sunset:
the wave
bends down its head,
a ghost-swan
or angel
spilling
feathers
below the cliffs

SERAPHIM

[c. 1224]

Brother Leo was walking with him once when he said, 'Go back
...' So he turned back ... Then he saw a parchment come down
from heaven upon the head of Francis and circle round his feet.
As Leo watched carefully, Francis saw the parchment and picked
it up ...

Verba Conradi (New Fioretti, p. 61)

While he was staying in the hermitage of La Verna, he saw in
vision a man, with six wings like a Seraph, standing over him,
arms extended and feet joined, fixed to a cross ... He was delighted
by the kind and gracious look the Seraph gave him, and the
angel's beauty was beyond comprehension, but the fact that he
was fixed to a cross ... thoroughly frightened him. He kept
wondering what it meant ...

Celano, Life 2, iii

The angels do not serve you yet.
They hover still
as sickles by a field, or clouds
behind the hill,

with viols well-tuned, in case your pain
cannot be borne,
to ease it out as from a wound
the stubborn thorn.

But you once saw an angel come
small among birds,
brittle as parchment, inked across
with unknown words,

and this you caught, a vellum dart
live in your hand;
but could not yet expound its wings,
or understand.

Firle Beacon
(*Incident reported in the* Daily Mirror,
8th November 1940)

Out on this ridge Fred Fowler saw a vision:
a cross, Christ, six robed seraphs, clear as day.
He wore thick glasses, but they did not trick him;
the shining figures did not fade away.

He saw the nails, Christ's feet pierced through and bleeding;
the feet too of the angels, cloudy white,
even their toes. And then he fell to wondering
if they had come to put this poor world right.

His sheep were undisturbed, though Bob and Watch ran
in slow bewildered courses to and fro,
searching the ground for where the light had fallen,
while still the midday-filling heavenly glow

poured on the village. Then Grace Evans saw it,
calling to rouse her sister Emily,
who came from pegging washing, red hands damply
designing harps and angels in the sky,

as Fred came down the hill, his old coat flapping,
feathered with bracken, bowler hat and crook
clamped into place, his flock as loud as ever,
and nothing out of usual in his look.

$\rightarrow$

He told the *Mirror* it was like a film show,
at least as film shows were described to him;
but much more real, what with that blaze, that glory.
The vicar said he had not seen a thing.

Angelic
messages
above the fields
in smoke-grey, pink, smeared gold,
resist
deciphering;
last crows
scratch through
impatient
glosses

STIGMATA

Although he was unable to make clear sense of the vision [at La Verna], its novelty pressed upon his heart. Signs of the nails began to appear on his hands and feet, just as he had seen them a little while earlier on the crucified man hovering over him.

His hands and feet seemed to be pierced through the middle by nails, with the heads of the nails appearing on the inner part of his hands and on the upper part of his feet, and their points protruding on opposite sides ... His right side was marked with an oblong scar, as if pierced with a lance, and this often dripped blood ...

He hid those marks carefully from strangers, and concealed them cautiously from people close to him ... fearing that if he showed them, he would lose some of the grace given to him.

Celano, *Life* 2, iii

So in the end He did not speak.
You've woken up
still in the dark, and shaking. In
your thin clay cup
there's water, but your hands are clenched
round scabs, round pain;
you spill it. To the east the sky
lightens again
where He has flown in beauty, where
you cry to go,
but cannot. Cautiously you stand,
although you know
with rising calm and love, that some
strange sacred stone
has lamed both spavined feet, as if
forced through the bone—

And when you touch your opened side,
warm trickling red
anoints your fingers. Just like this
He buckled, bled;

in this same wondrous way
you live, though dead.

The crypt, Santa Chiara, Assisi

Too close an intimacy with the dead
whisperingly disturbs us: musty store
of clothes left in a wardrobe, or the dry
box-tang of soap and pastilles in a drawer,
with underwear we quickly thrust away
in sealed-up bags. It is as if we fear
death's ring around our necks, its random flakes
upon our shoulders too—
     And yet, just here,
we find a small surprising thing of yours:
a stocking that concealed your bolted foot,
fresh-washed and ironed. No rusty blood, snagged thread
or any more disturbing proofs of good;
and yet this reached your thigh, your hidden skin,
white and unthought of. Now our phones embrace
too much of you—until the counter-flash
of glass that intercepts us, or of grace.

No turning
from this path
where the mist drops
and the walker
vanishes ahead—
where blackberries
mush to water,
dry thorn leaves
yellow and fade;
but the haws hang
full, wine, red.

SWEET DEATH

'Laudato si mi Signore, per sora nostra Morte corporale,
de la quale nullu homo vivente po skappare...
Be praised my Lord for our sister Bodily Death, which no man
living can escape ...'

Francis, Canticle of Brother Sun

'If I am going to die soon, call Brother Angelo and Brother Leo
to me that they may sing to me of Sister Death.'

Francis in Scripta Leonis, 100

During his last sickness, he sent to the lady Jacqueline di Settesoli
for 'some religious garment of colour like ashes, and with the cloth
she should send some of the sweetmeat she has often made for me
in [Rome].' [This was what the Romans call mostaccioli, *which*
is made of almonds and sugar and other things.] She brought both,
and he managed to eat a little of the mostaccioli...

Mirror of Perfection, 168

Here's wheaten flour, ground powder-fine
by mills along the tumbling streams
where you would sleep:
> your simple substance, sieved in dreams
> and sifted deep.

Here's egg-whites, gluey-thick, which cling
skin-close as your persistent lust
and vanity:
> beaten till past collapsing, glossed
> to purity.

Here's almonds, with their bitter oil
that could dissolve you; saffron strands,
sugar in grain:
> sweet mercy at His blessed hands,
> shell-crushing pain.

All these are mixed and put through fire,
then cooled, and in an ash-grey nap
parcelled up tight:
> so close that He will then unwrap
> nothing but light.

Brighton seafront, March

Past Krispy-Kreme feasters,
ice-cream dealers,
candy-floss blowers,
orange-peelers,
macaroon-nibblers,
winged bun-stealers,
Sprite-spilling bad lads,
licorice-wheelers,
mums downing alcopops,
heartburn-healers,

  they walk:
                two men in those black
particular coats,
neither long nor short, square-cut
for shouldering loads;
and we ask ourselves once more
who they are going for.

Far off, slow blows
of axe on tree
fill the rapt air
as solemnly
as church bells would,
swung through with prayer

CUT DOWN

3rd October 1226

At his death, he had himself placed naked on the naked ground.
Celano, *Remembrance of the Desire of a Soul* 2, clxii

*After his death ... his limbs, which had been stiff, became perfectly
loose, so that they could be moved about ... like those of some
lovely boy.*
Letter of Brother Elias *(New Fioretti, p. 81)*

*Larks are birds that are friends of the light and dread the shadows
of dark. But in the evening when Francis passed from this world
to Christ, when it was already nightfall, they gathered above the
roof of the house ... singing with tearful joy and joyful tears.*
Celano, *Treatise on the Miracles,* iv

Towards the end they laid you down
a withered tree upon the ground.

Pierced hollow now, you weighed no more
than bark around an empty core.

They sought, with orisons and psalms,
the branching blessing of your arms;

Then sprinkled round you ash and loam,
as trees and men must both become.

Yet where you lay your sinews made
an instrument that Heaven played;

and your dry limbs flexed light again
as leaves revived by dropping rain—

or by the tears of larks that flew
where angel wings were lifting you.

Larch wood, Powys

They left the birch and the hazel
single, or twos and threes
half-naked in mist-cold October,
the unguarded trees,

but of larches nothing remaining
save logs thrown here and there,
needles, twigs, splinters and absence
imprinted on the air,

grace gone, and the shimmering fall
of branch on branch downswinging;
the dance wrecked, and the dancers
stopped in their singing,

ghosts in the fog. They were diseased,
said the man who passed in the lane;
had to go, would not be replanted
on these slopes again,

for that was the fate of these larches:
to be lovely, to die.
And the rising sun where the wood was
reigns in an empty sky.

ENVOI

Basilica, La Verna

Where pilgrims mill and stare and photograph,
a young friar trots in with a watering-can
and genuflects. The lilies in their vase
need water, or they die, like any man.

Drab in the holidaying crowd, mute brown
as earth itself, he sinks upon his knees
before the leaves. For us, such falling down
may seem abasement; but for him the ease

of sandalled everyday. Above him, see,
against hard blue, slim shining lilies flower
in painted clay: immortal as he'll be
also, beyond this place, beyond this hour.

LIST OF SOURCES

Saint Bonaventure, *The Life of Saint Francis* (Temple Classics, Dent, London, 1932)

Brother Leo (attr.) *The Mirror of Perfection*, tr. from the Cottonian MS by Robert Steele (Dent, London, 1903)

Thomas di Celano, *The Francis Trilogy (The Life of Saint Francis, 1 and 2; Remembrance of the Desire of a Soul, 1 and 2; Treatise on the Miracles of Saint Francis)*, ed. Regis Armstrong, J.A. Wayne Hellmann and William J. Short (New City Press, New York, 2004)

Francis of Assisi: *The Complete Writings, with the Little Flowers of Saint Francis*. Z. El-Bey (illifeebooks@gmail.com, 2009)

The Legend of St Francis by the Three Companions, tr. E.G. Salter (Dent, London, 1902)

Scripta Leonis, Rufini et Angeli, Sociorum S. Francisci, ed. and tr. Rosalind B. Brooke (Oxford University Press, 1990)

A New Fioretti: A collection of early stories about Saint Francis hitherto untranslated, tr. John R.H. Moorman (SPCK, London, 1946)

Augustine Thompson, OP: *Francis of Assisi: A New Biography*. (Cornell University Press, Ithaca and London, 2012)

ACKNOWLEDGEMENTS

Warmest thanks to Mark Studer, who introduced me to Tuscany and Umbria and was a wonderful guide on several visits to the Franciscan sites. Thanks too to Peter Abbs, Lizzie Fincham, John Hendry, A.D. Miller and Joe Winter, for reading the manuscript and encouraging me in the enterprise.